How I Feel

I Feel Excited

By Connor Stratton

level
2
little blue
readers

www.littlebluehousebooks.com

Little Blue House is distributed by North Star Editions:
sales@northstareditions.com | 888-417-0195

Produced for Little Blue House by Red Line Editorial.

Photographs ©: Shutterstock Images, cover, 4, 15, 18, 21 (top), 21 (bottom), 22–23, 24 (top left), 24 (top right); iStockphoto, 7, 8–9, 11, 12, 16–17, 24 (bottom left), 24 (bottom right)

Library of Congress Control Number: 2020913844

ISBN
978-1-64619-296-0 (hardcover)
978-1-64619-314-1 (paperback)
978-1-64619-350-9 (ebook pdf)
978-1-64619-332-5 (hosted ebook)

Printed in the United States of America
Mankato, MN
012021

About the Author

Connor Stratton enjoys writing books for children and watching movies, such as *Inside Out*. He's always trying to understand his feelings better. He lives in Minnesota.

Table of Contents

playground

At the Playground

We are going to
the playground.
I feel excited.

I wait my turn to go down the slide.

I feel excited.

I know I will have fun.

slide

I am excited to play on the swings.

I have fun when I swing.

swing

I go to the sandbox, and I feel excited.

I play in the sand, and I have fun.

sand

At a Party

We are going to a party.

I feel excited.

There are treats at

the party.

The treats look good.

I am excited to eat them.

There are games at
the party.

The games look fun.

I am excited to play them.

game

grandparents

With My Family

We are going to see my grandparents.

I love my grandparents.

I feel excited.

My grandfather likes
to cook.

My grandmother likes to
play games.

I am excited to cook and
play games.

grandfather

grandmother

game

21

I read with
my grandparents.
I am excited to see
them again.

grandparents

Glossary

game

playground

grandparents

swings

Index